word building

At School

Word Building with Prefixes and Suffixes

Pam Scheunemann

Consulting Editor, Diane Craig, M.A./Reading Specialist

A Division of ABDO

ABDO
Publishing Company

visit us at www.abdopublishing.com

Published by ABDO Publishing Company, a division of ABDO, P.O. Box 398166, Minneapolis, Minnesota 55439. Copyright © 2013 by Abdo Consulting Group, Inc. International copyrights reserved in all countries. No part of this book may be reproduced in any form without written permission from the publisher. Super SandCastle™ is a trademark and logo of ABDO Publishing Company.

Printed in the United States of America, North Mankato, Minnesota
062012
092012

 PRINTED ON RECYCLED PAPER

Editor: Liz Salzmann
Content Developer: Nancy Tuminelly
Interior Design: Kelly Doudna, Mighty Media, Inc.
Production: Oona Gaarder-Juntti, Mighty Media, Inc.
Photo Credits: Brand X, Creatas Images, Dynamic Graphics, Jupiterimages, Photodisc, PhotoObjects.net, Shutterstock, Stockbyte, Thinkstock Images, Zedcor Wholly

Library of Congress Cataloging-in-Publication Data
Scheunemann, Pam, 1955-
  At school : word building with prefixes and suffixes / Pam Scheunemann.
     p. cm. -- (Word building)
  ISBN 978-1-61714-969-6
  1. English language--Suffixes and prefixes--Juvenile literature. 2. Vocabulary--Juvenile literature. 3. Language arts (Elementary) I. Title.
  PE1175.S323 2012
  428.1--dc22
                        2010054482

Super SandCastle™ books are created by a team of professional educators, reading specialists, and content developers around five essential components—phonemic awareness, phonics, vocabulary, text comprehension, and fluency—to assist young readers as they develop reading skills and strategies and increase their general knowledge. All books are written, reviewed, and leveled for guided reading, early reading intervention, and Accelerated Reader® programs for use in shared, guided, and independent reading and writing activities to support a balanced approach to literacy instruction.

contents

What is Word Building?

Word building is adding groups of letters to a word. The added letters change the word's meaning.

cover**s**

Prefix

Some groups of letters are added to the beginning of words. They are called prefixes. Some prefixes have more than one meaning.

Suffix

Some groups of letters are added to the end of words. They are called suffixes. Some suffixes have more than one meaning.

un + cover + ed

prefix + base word + suffix

uncovered

The prefix **un** means not or opposite.
The base word **cover** means to put something over
or on top of something else.
The suffix **ed** turns a word into an adjective.
Uncovered means that something does not have anything over it.

Let's Build words

read

Tommy likes to read with his dad.

Al rereads his favorite book.

6

Chandra is reading at the library.

reread s

The prefix **re** means to do it again.

The suffix **s** means that the action is happening now.

read ing

The suffix **ing** means that the action is happening now.

More Words

reads, reader, readers, reread, rereading

7

think

Ava likes to think before she writes.

Sally rethinks her first answer.

Marshall is thinking about his next move.

rethinks

The prefix **re** means to do it again.

The suffix **s** means that the action is happening now.

thinking

The suffix **ing** means that the action is happening now.

More words

thinks, thinker, thinkers, rethink, rethinking, unthinking, unthinkable

write

Brianna has a fun pen to write with.

Jess rewrites a note to her friend.

Andrew is writing down
the answers.

rewrites

The prefix **re** means to do
something again.

The suffix **s** means that the
action is happening now.

writing

The suffix **ing** means that
the action is happening now.

More Words

writes, writer, writers,
rewrite, rewriting, written,
unwritten, rewritten

RULE

When a verb ends with *e*, drop
the *e* before adding **ing**.

health

Jordan eats carrots to improve her health.

Max knows that eating pizza every day would be unhealthy.

Ted feels healthiest when he exercises every day.

unhealthy

The prefix **un** means not or opposite.

The suffix **y** turns a noun into an adjective.

healthiest

The suffix **est** means most.

More words

healthy, healthier, healthily, healthiness, unhealthier, unhealthiest, unhealthily, unhealthiness

᪥ ᪥ ᪥ Rule ᪥ ᪥ ᪥

When a word ends with *y*, change the *y* to *i* before adding **est**.

fold

Nan learns how to fold paper into birds.

Jasmine's arms are unfolded.

14

Mark is folding a paper airplane.

unfolded

The prefix **un** means not or opposite.

The suffix **ed** turns a word into an adjective.

folding

The suffix **ing** means that the action is happening now.

More words

folds, folded, unfold, foldable, unfoldable, folder, unfolder

The Repainted School

Jesse likes bright colors more than most.
He may even like to paint his toast!
It was nearly time to start back to school.
Jesse had an idea for something cool.

His school was painted a dark gray.
That color of paint kept the kids away.
Jesse wanted to paint the school bright.
Kids would want to go there even
at night!

He asked the teacher if his idea was okay.

She said, "Thanks for asking. You can start today!"

When the painting was done, people said, "Hooray!"

The school was repainted.

No more boring gray!

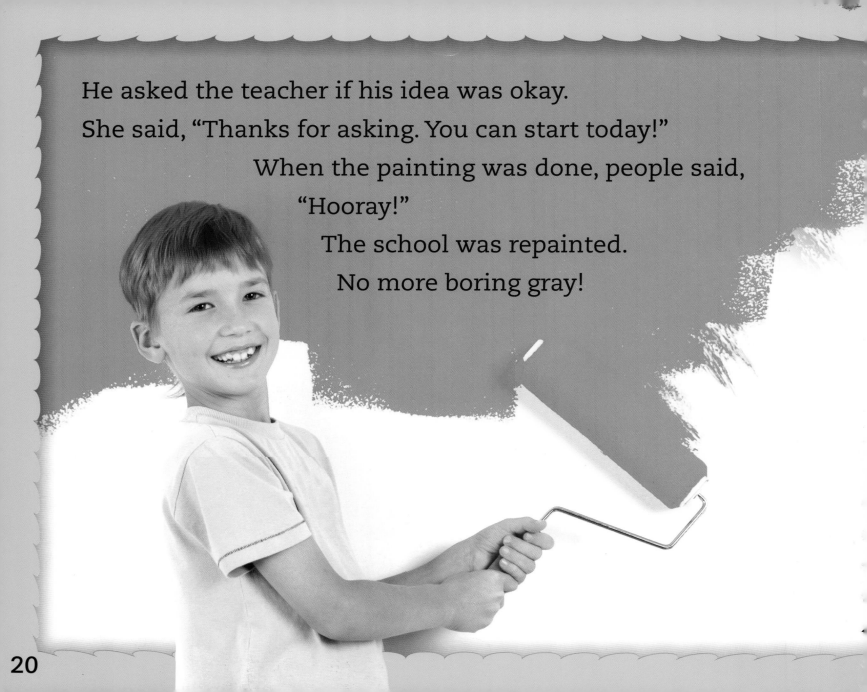

Match it up!

Choose the word with the correct prefix or suffix to complete each sentence.

1 Kayla is _____ a book.
   a. reading
   b. reads

2 Lauren _____ about lunch.
   a. thinks
   b. thinking

3 Barry is _____ the answers.
    a. writer
    b. rewriting

4 Ian likes to eat _____ foods.
    a. unhealthiness
    b. healthy

5 Rita has her arms _____.
    a. folded
    b. folding

Glossary

adjective (pp. 5, 13, 15) – a word used to describe someone or something. Tall, green, round, happy, and cold are all adjectives.

favorite (p. 6) – someone or something that you like best.

hooray (p. 20) – a word people yell when they are happy about something.

improve (p. 12) – to get or make better.

meaning (pp. 4, 5) – the idea or sense of something said or written.

noun (p. 13) – a word that is the name of a person, place, or thing.

opposite (pp. 5, 13, 15) – being completely different from another thing.

toast (p. 17) – bread that has been cooked so it is dry and brown.

verb (p. 11) – a word for an action. Be, do, think, play, and sleep are all verbs.